Dee,
Wishing you
peace of mind.
Merry Christmas.
Love,
Sara

P9-CDU-246

A Host of Angels

A Host of Angels

Edited by Gail Harvey

Gramercy Books
New York • Avenel

Introduction and Compilation
Copyright © 1992 by Random House Value Publishing, Inc.
All rights reserved

Published by Gramercy Books
distributed by Random House Value Publishing, Inc.,
40 Engelhard Avenue
Avenel, New Jersey 07001

Manufactured in the United States

Designed by Liz Trovato

Library of Congress Cataloging-in-Publication Data
A Host of angels.
p.   cm.
ISBN 0-517-08140-7
1. Angels—Quotations, maxims, etc.
PN6084.A55H67   1992
291.2'15—dc20   92-11394   CIP

12   11   10   9   8   7

$\mathcal{T}$he word *angel* comes from the Greek word for messenger; angels are messengers from God. They seem to speak every human language fluently, and, with the exception of the Angel of Death, they always seem to bring good news. Often, too, an angel will save someone from disaster.

A Host of Angels is a celebration of God's winged messengers. Dante gives a description of angels. Ralph Waldo Emerson explains under what circumstances an angel appears. Saint Augustine assures us that "Every visible thing in this world is put in the charge of an angel" and Emanuel Swedenborg writes of the great power of angels in the spiritual world.

Included, too, are excerpts from the Old and New Testaments, as well as from the Koran. And there are poems by such well-known writers as Christina Rossetti, John Greenleaf Whittier, William Blake, and W.B. Yeats.

This lovely book, with its enchanting illustrations, will surely delight everyone who has ever sensed, or wished for, an angelic presence.

GAIL HARVEY

New York
1992

ngels are spirits, but it is not because they are spirits that they are angels. They become angels when they are sent. For the name *angel* refers to their office, not their nature. You ask the name of this nature, it is *spirit*; you ask its office, it is that of an angel, which is a messenger.

SAINT AUGUSTINE

*Be not forgetful
to entertain strangers,
for thereby some have
entertained angels
unawares.*

HEBREWS 13:2

How shall we tell an angel
    From another guest?
How, from the common worldly herd,
    One of the blest?

Hint of suppressed halo,
    Rustle of hidden wings,
Wafture of heavenly frankincense,—
    Which is these things?

The old Sphinx smiles so subtly:
    "I give no golden rule,—
Yet I would warn thee, World: treat well
    Whom thou call'st fool."

GERTRUDE HALL

 passing Angel, speed me with a song,
A melody of heaven to reach my heart
And rouse me to the race and make me strong.

CHRISTINA ROSSETTI

I believe we are free, within limits, and yet there is an unseen hand, a guiding angel, that somehow, like a submerged propeller, drives us on.

RABINDRANATH TAGORE

*F*or He shall give His angels charge over thee, to keep thee in all thy ways.

They shall bear thee up in their hands, lest thou dash thy foot against a stone.

PSALM 91:11-12

God called the nearest angels who dwell
    with Him above:
The tenderest one was Pity, the dearest one
    was Love.

"Arise," He said, "my angels! a wail of
    woe and sin
Steals through the gates of heaven, and
    saddens all within.

"My harps take up the mournful strain
    that from a lost world swells,
The smoke of torment clouds the light and
    blights the asphodels.

"Fly downward to that under world, and
    on its souls of pain
Let Love drop smiles like sunshine, and
    Pity tears like rain!"

Two faces bowed before the Throne, veiled
    in their golden hair;
Four white wings lessened swiftly down the
    dark abyss of air.

The way was strange, the flight was long;
    at last the angels came

Where swung the lost and nether world,
  red-wrapped in rayless flame.

There Pity, shuddering, wept; but Love,
  with faith too strong for fear,
Took heart from God's almightiness and
  smiled a smile of cheer.

And lo! that tear of Pity quenched the
  flame whereon it fell,
And, with the sunshine of that smile, hope
  entered into hell!

Two unveiled faces full of joy looked upward
  to the Throne,
Four white wings folded at the feet of Him
  who sat thereon!

And deeper than the sound of seas, more
  soft than falling flake,
Amidst the hush of wing and song the
  Voice Eternal spake:

"Welcome, my angels! ye have brought a
  holier joy to heaven;
Henceforth its sweetest song shall be the
  song of sin forgiven!"

JOHN GREENLEAF WHITTIER

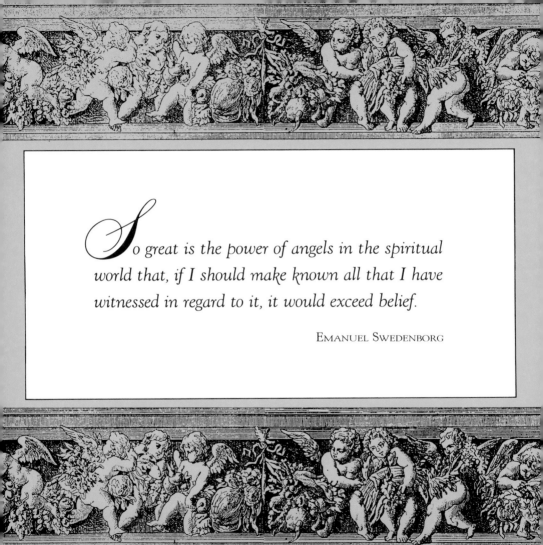

*S*o great is the power of angels in the spiritual world that, if I should make known all that I have witnessed in regard to it, it would exceed belief.

EMANUEL SWEDENBORG

It is not because angels are holier than men or devils that makes them angels, but because they do not expect holiness from one another, but from God alone.

WILLIAM BLAKE

usic is well said
to be the speech of angels.

THOMAS CARLYLE

Their faces were living flame, their wings were gold, and for the rest, their white was so intense, no snow can match the white they showed. . . . From rank to rank, they shared that peace and ardor which they gained with wings that fanned their sides.

DANTE

The angel Israfel,
whose heartstrings are a lute,
has the sweetest voice of all
God's creatures.

THE KORAN

The angel Gabriel was sent from God unto a city of Galilee, named Nazareth.

To a virgin espoused to a man whose name was Joseph, of the house of David; and the virgin's name was Mary.

And the angel came in unto her, and said, Hail, thou that art highly favored, the Lord is with thee: blessed art thou among women.

LUKE 1:26-28

There were...shepherds abiding in the field, keeping watch over their flock by night.

And, lo, the angel of the Lord came upon them, and the glory of the Lord shone round about them, and they were sore afraid.

And the angel said unto them, "Fear not, for behold, I bring you good tidings of great joy, which shall be to all people.

For unto you is born this day in the city of David, a savior, which is Christ the Lord.

LUKE 2:8-11

Hark! the herald angels sing,—
"Glory to the newborn King!
Peace on earth, and mercy mild,
God and sinners reconciled."
Joyful, all ye nations, rise.
Join the triumph of the skies;
With th' angelic host proclaim,
"Christ is born in Bethlehem."
Hark! the herald angels sing,
"Glory to the newborn King!"

CHARLES WESLEY

Angels, from the realms of glory,
  Wing your flight o'er all the earth;
Ye, who sang creation's story,
  Now proclaim Messiah's birth.
    Come and worship! Come and worship!
    Worship Christ the newborn King!

Shepherds, in the fields abiding,
  Watching o'er your flocks by night,
God with man is now residing,
  Yonder shines the infant light.
    Come and worship! Come and worship!
    Worship Christ the newborn King!

Sages, leave your contemplations,
  Brighter visions beam afar;
Seek the great Desire of nations,
  Ye have seen his natal star.
    Come and worship! Come and worship!
    Worship Christ the newborn King!

All creation, join in praising
  God, the Father, Spirit, Son,
Evermore your voices raising
  To the eternal Three in One.
    Come and worship! Come and worship!
    Worship Christ the newborn King!

CHRISTMAS CAROL

*I*f I have freedom in my love,
And in my soul am free,
Angels alone that soar above
Enjoy such liberty.

Richard Lovelace

It came upon a midnight clear,
That glorious song of old,
From angels bending near the earth
To touch their harps of gold.

"Peace on the earth, good will to men,
From Heav'n's all-gracious King!"
The world in solemn stillness lay
To hear the angels sing.

Still through the cloven skies they come,
With peaceful wings unfurl'd,
And still their heav'nly music floats
O'er all the weary world;

Above its sad and lowly plains
They bend on hov'ring wing,
And ever o'er its Babel sounds
The blessed angels sing.

For lo! the days are hastening on
By prophets seen of old
When with the evercircling years,
Shall come the time foretold,

When the new heav'n and earth shall own
The Prince of Peace their King,
And the whole world send back the song
Which now the angels sing.

EDMUND H. SEARS

It is in rugged crises, in unweariable endurance, and in aims which put sympathy out of the question, that the angel is shown.

RALPH WALDO EMERSON

Every visible thing in this world is put in the charge of an angel.

SAINT AUGUSTINE

Christians, awake, salute the happy morn,
Whereon the Savior of the world was born.
Rise to adore the mystery of love,
Which hosts of Angels chanted from above.

*o love for the sake of
being loved is human,
but to love for the
sake of loving is angelic.*

ALPHONSE DE LAMARTINE

Twice or thrice had I loved thee,
Before I knew thy face or name.
So in a voice, so in a shapeless flame,
Angels affect us oft, and worshipped be.

JOHN DONNE

I dreamt a Dream! what can it mean?
And that I was a maiden Queen.
Guarded by an Angel mild:
Witless woe was ne'er beguil'd!

And I wept both night and day,
And he wip'd my tears away,
And I wept both day and night,
And hid from him my heart's delight.

So he took his wings and fled;
Then the morn blush'd rosy red;
I dried my tears then, & arm'd my fears
With ten thousand shields and spears.

Soon my Angel came again:
I was arm'd, he came in vain;
For the time of youth was fled,
And gray hairs were on my head.

WILLIAM BLAKE

There was a pause—just long enough for an angel to pass, flying slowly.

RONALD FIRBANK

*A*ngels can fly
because they take
themselves lightly.

G. K. Chesterton

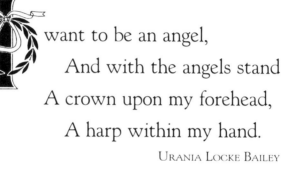 want to be an angel,
  And with the angels stand
  A crown upon my forehead,
  A harp within my hand.

URANIA LOCKE BAILEY

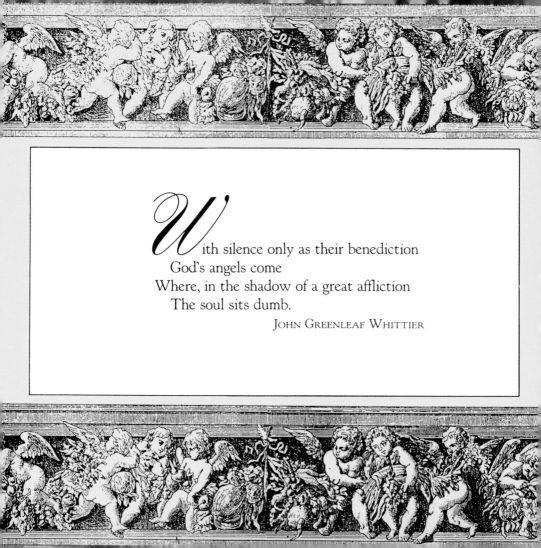

With silence only as their benediction
   God's angels come
Where, in the shadow of a great affliction
   The soul sits dumb.

JOHN GREENLEAF WHITTIER

I am well aware that many will say that no one can possibly speak with spirits and angels so long as he is living in the body; many say it is all fancy, others that I recount such things to win credence, while others will make other kinds of objection. But I am deterred by none of these: for I have seen, I have heard, I have felt.

EMANUEL SWEDENBORG

The angels keep their ancient places;
Turn but a stone, and start a wing!
'Tis ye, 'tis your estranged faces,
That miss the many-splendored thing.

FRANCIS THOMPSON

Jacob dreamed, and behold, a ladder set up on the earth, and the top of it reached to Heaven; and behold the angels of God ascending and descending on it.

GENESIS 28:12

*For a good angel will go with him,
his journey will be successful, and he will
come home safe and sound.*

APOCRYPHA, TOBIAS 5:21

And nd yet, as angels in some brighter dreams
Call to the soul when man doth sleep,
So some strange thoughts transcend our wonted themes,
And into glory peep.

HENRY VAUGHAN

The angels are stooping
Above your bed;
They weary of trooping
With the whimpering dead.

God's laughing in heaven
To see you so good;
The Shining Seven
Are gay with His mood.

I kiss you and kiss you,
My pigeon, my own;
Ah, how I shall miss you
When you have grown.

W. B. YEATS

*A*ngels at the foot,
And Angels at the head,
And like a curly little lamb
My pretty babe in bed.

CHRISTINA ROSSETTI

Hush my dear, lie still and slumber!
Holy angels guard thy bed!
Heavenly blessings without number
Gently falling on thy head.

ISAAC WATTS

Matthew, Mark, Luke, and John
The bed be blessed that I lie on.
Four angels to my bed,
Four angels round my head,
One to watch, and one to pray,
And two to bear my soul away.

AUTHOR UNKNOWN